GOODBYE, MR HOLLYWOOD

'The girl suddenly took Nick's face between her hands, and kissed him on the mouth. "Drive carefully, Mr Hollywood. Goodbye," she said, with a big, beautiful smile. Then she turned and walked quickly away.'

Nick Lortz doesn't understand. He only met the girl ten minutes ago when she came and sat next to him in the café. So why does she kiss him when she leaves? And why does she call him 'Mr Hollywood'? He thinks about these questions when he is driving to Vancouver, but he doesn't find the answers. And there is one more thing that Nick doesn't know.

Somebody is listening when the girl says goodbye to him – somebody who is very interested in the name 'Mr Hollywood'. And in Vancouver Nick soon learns that it's not a friendly interest . . .

OXFORD BOOKWORMS LIBRARY
Thriller & Adventure

Goodbye, Mr Hollywood

Stage 1 (400 headwords)

Series Editor: Jennifer Bassett
Founder Editor: Tricia Hedge
Activities Editors: Jennifer Bassett and Alison Baxter

JOHN ESCOTT

Goodbye,
Mr Hollywood

OXFORD UNIVERSITY PRESS

OXFORD
UNIVERSITY PRESS

Great Clarendon Street, Oxford OX2 6DP

Oxford University Press is a department of the University of Oxford.
It furthers the University's objective of excellence in research, scholarship,
and education by publishing worldwide in

Oxford New York

Auckland Cape Town Dar es Salaam Hong Kong Karachi
Kuala Lumpur Madrid Melbourne Mexico City Nairobi
New Delhi Shanghai Taipei Toronto

With offices in

Argentina Austria Brazil Chile Czech Republic France Greece
Guatemala Hungary Italy Japan Poland Portugal Singapore
South Korea Switzerland Thailand Turkey Ukraine Vietnam

OXFORD and OXFORD ENGLISH are registered trade marks of
Oxford University Press in the UK and in certain other countries

ISBN 978 0 19 478905 9

A complete recording of this Bookworms edition of
Goodbye, Mr Hollywood is available on audio CD ISBN 978 0 19 478840 3

Printed in Hong Kong

ACKNOWLEDGEMENTS
Illustrated by: Paul Dickinson

Word count (main text): 5200 words

For more information on the Oxford Bookworms Library,
visit www.oup.com/bookworms

CONTENTS

— 1 —

Mystery girl

It all began on a beautiful spring morning in a village called Whistler, in Canada – a pretty little village in the mountains of British Columbia.

There was a café in the village, with tables outside, and at one of these tables sat a young man. He finished his breakfast, drank his coffee, looked up into the blue sky, and felt the warm sun on his face. Nick Lortz was a happy man.

The waiter came up to his table. 'More coffee?' he asked.

'Yeah. Great,' said Nick. He gave the waiter his coffee cup.

The waiter looked at the camera on the table. 'On vacation?' he said. 'Where are you from?'

'On vacation?'

'San Francisco,' Nick said. He laughed. 'But I'm not on vacation – I'm working. I'm a travel writer, and I'm doing a book on mountains in North America. I've got some great pictures of your mountain.'

The two men looked up at Whistler Mountain behind the village. It looked very beautiful in the morning sun.

'Do you travel a lot, then?' asked the waiter.

'All the time,' Nick said. 'I write books, and I write for travel magazines. I write about everything – different countries, towns, villages, rivers, mountains, people . . .'

The waiter looked over Nick's head. 'There's a girl across the street,' he said. 'Do you know her?'

Nick turned his head and looked. 'No, I don't.'

'Well, she knows you, I think,' the waiter said. 'She's watching you very carefully.' He gave Nick a smile. 'Have a nice day!' He went away, back into the café.

Nick looked at the girl across the street. She was about twenty-five, and she was very pretty. 'She *is* watching me,' Nick thought. Then the girl turned and looked in one of the shop windows. After a second or two, she looked back at Nick again.

Nick watched her. 'She looks worried,' he thought. 'What's she doing? Is she waiting for somebody?'

Suddenly, the girl smiled. Then she walked across the street, came up to Nick's table, and sat down. She put her bag down on the table. The bag was half-open.

2

The girl came up to Nick's table.

'Hi! I'm Jan,' she said. 'Do you remember me? We met at a party in Toronto.'

'Hi, Jan,' said Nick. He smiled. 'I'm Nick. But we didn't meet at a party in Toronto. I don't go to parties very often, and never in Toronto.'

'Oh,' the girl said. But she didn't get up or move away.

'Have some coffee,' said Nick. The story about the party in Toronto wasn't true, but it was a beautiful morning, and she was a pretty girl. 'Maybe it was a party in Montréal. Or New York.'

The girl laughed. 'OK. Maybe it was. And yes, I'd love some coffee.'

When she had her coffee, Nick asked, 'What are you doing in Whistler? Or do you live here?'

'Oh no,' she said. 'I'm just, er, just travelling through. And what are *you* doing here?'

'I'm a travel writer,' Nick said, 'and I'm writing a book about famous mountains.'

'That's interesting,' she said. But her face was worried, not interested, and she looked across the road again.

A man with very short, white hair walked across the road. He was about sixty years old, and he was tall and thin. The girl watched him.

'Are you waiting for someone?' asked Nick.

'No,' she said quickly. Then she asked, 'Where are you going next, Nick?'

'To Vancouver, for three or four days,' he said.

'When are you going?' she asked.

'Later this morning,' he said. There was a letter in the top of the girl's half-open bag. Nick could see some of the writing, and he read it because he saw the word

'Vancouver' – . . . *and we can meet at the Empress Hotel,*
Victoria, Vancouver Island, on Friday afternoon . . .

'So she's going to Vancouver too,' he thought.

Suddenly the girl said, 'Do you like movies?'

'Movies? Yes, I love movies,' he said. 'Why?'

'I know a man, and he – he loves movies, and going to
the cinema,' she said slowly. 'People call him "Mr

'Are you waiting for someone?' asked Nick.

5

Hollywood".' She smiled at Nick. 'Can I call you "Mr Hollywood" too?'

Nick laughed. 'OK,' he said. 'And what can I call you?'

She smiled again. 'Call me Mystery Girl,' she said.

'That's a good name for you,' said Nick.

Just then, the man with white hair came into the café. He did not look at Nick or the girl, but he sat at a table near them. He asked the waiter for some breakfast, then he began to read a magazine.

The girl looked at the man, then quickly looked away again.

'Do you know him?' Nick asked her.

'No,' she said. She finished her coffee quickly and got up. 'I must go now,' she said.

Nick stood up, too. 'Nice to—' he began.

But the girl suddenly took his face between her hands, and kissed him on the mouth. 'Drive carefully, Mr Hollywood. Goodbye,' she said, with a big, beautiful smile. Then she turned and walked quickly away.

Nick sat down again and watched her. She walked down the road and into a big hotel.

'Now what,' thought Nick, 'was *that* all about?'

*   *   *

The man with white hair watched Nick and waited. After four or five minutes, Nick finished his coffee, took his books and his camera, and left the café. His car was just outside

'Drive carefully, Mr Hollywood.'

the girl's hotel, and he walked slowly along the street to it.

The man with white hair waited a second, then quickly followed Nick.

From a window high up in the hotel, the girl looked down into the road. She saw Nick, and the man with white hair about fifty yards behind him. Nick got into his car, and the man with white hair walked quickly to a red car across the street. Five seconds later Nick drove away in his blue car, and the red car began to follow him.

When the girl saw this, she smiled, then went to put some things in her travel bag.

*The man with white hair walked quickly
to a red car across the street.*

— 2 —

A hand in the back

That evening, in his hotel room in Vancouver, Nick could not stop thinking about the girl in the Whistler café. Why did she come and sit with him? She didn't know him, and that story about a party in Toronto wasn't true. And she was worried about something. But what?

And that kiss! It was nice, of course, but why did she do it? 'Maybe she liked my face,' Nick thought. 'Or my brown eyes. But I'm not going to see her again, so it doesn't matter. Forget it.'

He put some money in his pocket and went downstairs to the hotel restaurant. But there were no free tables, so he walked down to Gastown and found a restaurant there.

After dinner, he went for a walk. Vancouver was a friendly city, and Nick liked walking through Gastown and Chinatown, looking in the shops and watching the people. It was nearly dark now, and it was a busy time of the evening. There were a lot of cars, and a lot of people.

After a time, Nick began to walk back to his hotel. He came to a busy street, and waited, with a small crowd of people, to go across. A tall woman in a blue dress stood next to him. She turned and smiled at him.

'It's the first warm evening of spring,' she said. 'It's nice to be out, after the long cold winter.'

'Yeah,' said Nick. 'It's great. It's—'

Suddenly, there was a hand in his back – and the hand pushed Nick into the road. Nick fell on his face, in front of a big green car.

People screamed.

But the green car stopped, only inches from Nick's head. The woman in the blue dress ran into the road and pulled Nick to his feet.

'Are you OK? What happened?' she said.

The driver of the green car shouted angrily at Nick, but Nick did not hear him.

Nick fell on his face, in front of a big green car.

'Somebody pushed me,' he said to the woman. 'I didn't fall – somebody pushed me!'

'Pushed you?' said the woman. 'Who? I didn't see anybody.'

Nick looked at the faces of the people near him, but he didn't know them.

Then he saw a man's back. The man was tall and thin, and had very short white hair. He walked quickly away down the street, and did not look back.

'Hey, you!' Nick shouted. 'Wait!'

But the man did not stop, and he was soon lost in the crowds.

'Did *he* push you?' asked the woman in the blue dress.

11

'I . . . I don't know,' Nick said.

'Do you know him?' she asked.

'I don't know his name,' Nick said. 'But I know that short white hair. Now where did I see it before?'

The woman began to move away. 'I must get home,' she said. 'Are you OK now?'

'Yeah, I'm OK,' Nick said. 'And thanks. Thanks for your help.'

'That's OK.' The woman smiled. 'Be careful now!'

*   *   *

Back in his hotel, Nick sat on his bed and thought. 'It was an accident. Nobody pushed me, it was an accident. Nobody wants to kill me. And there are hundreds of men in Vancouver with white hair.'

It was one o'clock in the morning, but Nick couldn't sleep. He listened to the cars in the road, and he looked at the night sky through his hotel room window.

Then he sat at the table and tried to write some more of his book about mountains, but he couldn't think about his work. He got back into bed.

There were four or five magazines in the hotel room. They were not very interesting, but Nick sat in bed and opened one . . . *and saw a photo of 'Mystery Girl'!*

He looked at the picture very carefully. But, yes, it was her! Jan, the girl from the Whistler café.

She was next to a man of about fifty or fifty-five, and

12

Nick sat in bed and opened one . . . and saw a photo of 'Mystery Girl'!

they were in the garden of a big, expensive house. They smiled at the camera, and they looked very happy.

Canadian millionaire, Howard Hutson, and his daughter, Meg, it said under the picture, *at their home in Toronto*. Meg Hutson! Not Jan. Not Mystery Girl. Meg Hutson, the daughter of a millionaire! Nick read it again.

'Why did she come and sit with *me* in the café at Whistler?' he thought. 'Millionaires' daughters don't sit with strangers in cafés, and then give them a big kiss when they leave! Why did she do it? What did she want?'

*   *   *

He thought back to the café in Whistler, and the girl next to him at the table. Then he remembered something. He remembered a man at a table near them in the café. A tall thin man, about sixty years old. A man with very short white hair.

Nick didn't sleep much that night.

— **3** —

A walk in the park

The next day was Thursday. Nick stayed in his hotel room and wrote about mountains all morning. Then he drove to Stanley Park in the afternoon. He sat and read a book for an hour, then he went for a walk under the tall trees.

There was nobody here. It was quiet, and he could walk and think. He thought about Meg Hutson, and about the man with white hair. Did he know Meg Hutson? Did she know him? He remembered Meg Hutson's last words. *Drive carefully, Mr Hollywood.*

Why did she say that? Why did she call him Mr Hollywood? He didn't understand any of it.

Suddenly, he heard a noise.

Nick turned and ran.

He stopped. 'That was a gun!' he thought. 'There's somebody in the trees with a gun! There it is again!'

Then something hit the tree over his head.

'Somebody's shooting at me!' Nick thought. He turned and ran.

And somebody began to run after him.

Nick ran through the trees. There was no sun in here, and it was half-dark. And there were no people. Nobody to help him.

'I must get to my car,' Nick thought. 'Find some people . . . the police . . .' He ran on.

He could still hear the gunman behind him, so he ran faster. After three or four minutes, he stopped and listened.

Nothing. It was all quiet.

Nick was afraid. 'What's happening?' he thought. 'Why is somebody shooting at me? First a hand pushes me in front of a car, and now somebody's shooting at me!'

He waited another second or two, then walked quickly back to his car. He was very careful. He looked and listened all the time. But nobody came out of the trees, and nobody shot at him. Then he saw people – women with young children, some boys with a football, two men with a dog. He began to feel better. 'Nobody can shoot me now,' he thought. 'Not with all these people here.'

Ten minutes later, he was back at his car.

There was a letter on the window. Nick read it. It said: *I'm going to kill you, Mr Hollywood.*

* * *

Nick drove to the nearest police station. He waited for half an hour, then a tired young policeman took him into a small room. Nick told his story, and the policeman wrote it all down.

16

'How many people are there in this town with guns?'

'So what are you going to do?' asked Nick.

'Nothing,' said the policeman.

'Nothing!' said Nick. 'But somebody shot at me, and—'

'Mr Lortz,' the policeman said tiredly. 'How many people are there in this town with guns?'

'I don't know,' said Nick. 'But . . .'

'You didn't see the gunman. Was it a man, a boy, a woman? Colour of eyes? Long hair, short hair? You don't know, because you didn't see anybody. Maybe it was an

17

old girlfriend. Maybe somebody doesn't like your travel books, Mr Lortz.'

'But what about the man with white hair in Whistler?' said Nick. 'The girl, Meg Hutson, called me Mr Hollywood in the café, and this man heard her. And now I get a letter to Mr Hollywood on *my* car. Who *is* this Mr Hollywood?'

'We all want answers to our questions, Mr Lortz,' the policeman said, 'but we don't always get them.'

Questions. But no answers.

Nick walked out of the police station and drove to his hotel. He was angry, and afraid.

'How did the man with white hair find me in Vancouver?' he thought. 'Did he follow me from Whistler? Is he following me now? Maybe he's staying at my hotel, too. In the next room. With his gun.'

— **4** —

The man with white hair

Nick stopped his car in front of the hotel. He looked carefully before he got out, but there was nobody with white hair near the hotel.

He half-ran through the hotel doors and went to the desk inside.

'I'm looking for a man with very short white hair,' he

'It's very important. Please help me!'

said to the woman behind the desk. 'He's staying here, I think. He's about sixty years old, and he's tall and thin.'

The woman did not look very interested. 'There are a lot of visitors in the hotel,' she said. 'Do you know his name?'

'No, I don't,' Nick said. 'He's, er, a friend of a friend, you see. He arrived in Vancouver yesterday, and I must find him. It's very important. Please help me!'

The woman looked at him. 'There are three hundred and fifty rooms in this hotel,' she said, 'and maybe thirty or forty men with white hair. How can I remember all their

19

names?' She turned away to answer a telephone call.

Nick walked away from the desk.

'A drink,' he thought. 'I need a drink.' He went into the hotel bar, got a drink and sat down at a table.

'So what do I do now?' he thought.

And then he remembered something. A letter in the girl's half-open bag in the Whistler café.

... and we can meet at the Empress Hotel, Victoria, Vancouver Island, on Friday afternoon ...

And tomorrow was Friday.

'I'm going to Victoria, on Vancouver Island!' he thought. 'To the Empress Hotel!'

* * *

The boy and Nick fell down on the floor.

Nick had dinner in the hotel that evening. He finished eating and got up from his table . . . *and saw the man with white hair*.

Nick moved quickly. The man was at the hotel desk. Nick could see the white head above the other heads near the desk.

'Excuse me!' said Nick. He pushed past the people in the hotel restaurant. A small boy ran in front of him and Nick ran into him. The boy and Nick fell down on the floor. The boy began to cry.

'Hey!' said a woman behind Nick.

'I'm very sorry!' said Nick. He got up and helped the

boy to his feet. 'Are you OK?' he asked the boy.

'Be more careful next time,' said the woman.

Nick moved away quickly, but when he looked back at the hotel desk, he couldn't see the man with white hair. He pushed through the crowd of people.

'That man!' he shouted at the woman behind the desk. 'That man with short white hair. Where did he go?'

The woman looked at Nick. 'Mr Vickers?' she said. 'I don't know.'

'Vickers? Is that his name?' said Nick. 'What's his room number?'

'I'm sorry, I can't tell you that,' the woman said.

'But I need to—' began Nick.

The woman turned away to answer the telephone.

After a second or two, Nick went upstairs to his room.

'Vickers,' he thought. 'Does Meg Hutson know Mr Vickers? I need some answers, and I need them quickly!'

— 5 —

Vancouver Island

Tsawwassen was about twenty-three miles south of Vancouver. Nick drove there in his car the next morning for the one o'clock ferry to Vancouver Island. Every five minutes, he looked behind him. The road was busy – black cars, white cars, red cars, green cars. Maybe Vickers was in one of them.

At Tsawwassen Nick drove his car on to the ferry. There were a lot of cars and crowds of people. Nick got out of his car and walked up and down the ship. He looked for a man with white hair but he didn't see one.

He looked for a man with white hair but he didn't see one.

Soon the ferry began to move and Nick felt better. He found the ferry restaurant and got something to eat. More people came in. Nick looked at the faces of all the older men. Some had hats on, so he looked for somebody tall and thin, but there was nobody.

'Maybe he's not on the ferry,' Nick thought. 'Maybe he's back in Vancouver.'

Later, Nick walked around the ship again. Once, he thought he saw the man with white hair in the crowds, but he could not be sure.

Ninety minutes after leaving Tsawwassen, the ferry arrived at Swartz Bay on Vancouver Island, and Nick went back down to his car.

Swartz Bay was twenty miles north of Victoria. Nick drove quickly, and again, looked behind him every four or five minutes. Once, he saw a red car about two hundred yards behind him.

'Did I see that car on the road from Vancouver to Tsawwassen?' he thought.

He drove more slowly, but the red car still stayed two hundred yards behind him, and Nick couldn't see the driver's face or hair.

Soon he was in the busy streets of Victoria, and Nick didn't see the red car behind him again.

Victoria was a city of gardens and beautiful old buildings. Nick liked Victoria very much, but today he

'This is her.'

wasn't interested in gardens or buildings.

He found the Empress Hotel, went inside and walked across to the desk.

'Can I help you?' a young man asked Nick.

'I'm meeting a friend here this afternoon,' said Nick. 'Miss Hutson.'

'Hutson?' said the young man. 'Wait a minute.' He went away and came back. 'Sorry, but there's no Miss Hutson staying here.'

Nick took something from his pocket. It was the photograph of Meg and her father, from the magazine. 'This is her,' he said.

The young man looked at the picture. 'Oh, right. You mean Howard Hutson's daughter,' he said. 'She's not staying here, but I saw her ten or fifteen minutes ago. She was with somebody – a man. He asked me about the tea room.'

'The tea room?' said Nick. 'Where's that?'

* * *

The man with short white hair was tired. He couldn't sleep and he couldn't eat. He thought about only one thing, all the time. He drove and he watched, and he waited and he followed.

When he drove into Victoria, the streets were busy, and suddenly he lost the blue car in front of him. Angrily, he drove around the city, past all the big hotels. 'I must find him,' he said. 'I must do it. Today.'

Then he saw the Empress Hotel, and in the street outside it, a blue car.

He drove past the hotel, left his car, and ran back down the street. He went across the road and walked past the downstairs windows. There was a big room with tables and chairs, and a lot of people. He looked carefully at all the faces.

'There she is!' he said suddenly.

There were two men with the girl. He couldn't see their faces, only the backs of their heads, but one of the men was in a green shirt.

'Mr Hollywood,' the man said, and smiled. 'Goodbye, Mr Hollywood.' People in the street turned to look at him, but the man did not see them.

He walked up to the doors of the hotel and put a hand into his pocket. Inside, the gun was cold and hard.

'Goodbye, Mr Hollywood.'

— 6 —

A tea party

Nick looked through the doors of the tea room in the Empress Hotel.

Meg Hutson sat at a table with a man. The man was about thirty, or maybe a year or two younger. He was tall, and brown from the sun. He wore a white shirt, white

Meg Hutson sat at a table with a man.

trousers, and white shoes. He said something to Meg, and she laughed. She looked very happy.

A waiter came up to Nick. 'Can I get you some tea?' he asked.

'No, thanks,' said Nick. 'I'm with the two people over there.' And he walked across to Meg's table.

'Hello, Mystery Girl,' said Nick. 'Remember me? We met at Whistler. Your name was Jan then. But maybe today it's Meg Hutson.'

Meg Hutson looked up at him. 'Oh,' she said, and her face went red.

'Who is this, Meg?' asked the man.

'This is Nick,' said Meg. 'He's a writer. Nick, this is Craig Winters.'

'Sometimes called Mr Hollywood?' said Nick.

'Maybe. But how did *you* know that?' asked Craig Winters.

'I guessed,' said Nick. 'And I think I'm beginning to understand. Can I ask you a question, Mr Winters? Does somebody want to kill you?'

Craig Winters' face went white. 'Kill me?'

'What are you talking about?' asked Meg.

'Before I tell you, answer this question, please,' said Nick. 'You called *me* Mr Hollywood in Whistler. And you wanted the man at the next table, the man with white hair, to hear you. Is that right?'

'I wanted him to follow you, and not me.'

Meg Hutson did not answer at first. Then she said quietly, 'Yes.'

'Why?' asked Nick.

'I wanted him to follow you, and not me.'

'Why?' Nick asked again.

'I think he's a detective,' said Meg. 'And I think he's working for my father. I saw him soon after I left Toronto. He followed me.' Meg put her hand on Craig Winters' arm.

30

'My father doesn't like Craig. A month ago, he told me not to see Craig again. I'm not happy, and he knows that. I think he guessed that I'm meeting Craig. And now he wants to find Craig and stop him seeing me.'

'Stop him?' said Nick. 'Or kill him?'

'No!' Meg Hutson said. 'Daddy doesn't—'

'The man with white hair pushed me in front of a car in Vancouver,' Nick told her. 'And he shot at me in Stanley Park.'

'What!' said Meg.

'Tell – tell me about this man with white hair,' Winters said suddenly.

Nick looked at him. 'He's about sixty, and he's tall and thin,' he said.

'Do you know his name?' asked Winters.

'Vickers,' said Nick.

Craig Winters suddenly looked ill. 'Did he – did he follow you to Victoria? Did he follow you here?'

'I don't know,' said Nick. He watched Winters. 'You're afraid of him. Why? Why does this man Vickers want to kill you, Winters?'

Before Craig Winters could answer, Meg's face went white. 'Oh, no!' she said. 'Look! Look over there, by the door!'

Nick and Craig Winters turned to look. At the door of the tea room stood the man with white hair. He looked up and down the room, and then he saw them, and began to walk across to their table. His hand was in his pocket.

For a second or two the three people at the table did not move. Then Craig Winters jumped to his feet. 'That's Mr Hollywood!' he screamed. 'That man there!' And he pointed at Nick.

The man's hand came out of his pocket – with a gun. 'This is for Anna!' he shouted.

'This is for Anna!' he shouted.

Nick moved very fast. The tea table went over, and Nick was down on the floor in a second. The shot went over his head, and Meg screamed. At the same time Craig Winters shouted out and put a hand on his arm. There was blood on his white shirt. Then more people began to scream, and two waiters pulled the man with white hair down on to the floor.

'Get the police!' somebody shouted.

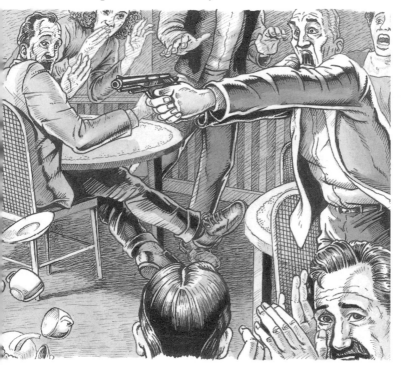

7

At the police station

It was 7.30 p.m. Nick and Meg were in a room at the police station. The man called Vickers was in a different room, with three detectives. There was a doctor with him too. Craig Winters was at the hospital.

The door opened and a detective came in with two cups of coffee. He put them down on the table, and turned to go out again.

'Detective Edmonds,' Meg said, 'did the hospital call? Is Craig going to be all right?'

'Winters?' Detective Edmonds said. 'Yes, he's going to be OK.'

'Can I call the hospital now?' asked Meg.

'I'd like you to wait,' said Edmonds. 'Detective Keat is going to be here in a minute. He's just coming from the airport and—' He looked through the open door. 'Ah, here he is now.'

A second detective came into the room, and behind him was a tall man with dark hair.

Meg stood up quickly. 'Daddy!' she cried. 'What are you doing here?'

'The police called me,' said Howard Hutson, 'and I flew

here at once. Detective Keat met me at the airport. Now, sit down, Meg. I want you to listen to me.' He did not look at Nick.

Meg sat down and her father took her hands. 'Meg, last week Johnnie Vickers came to my house. He wanted to talk about his daughter. You remember Anna, Meg? Three months ago she jumped off a bridge in Boston and died. She was young, beautiful, rich – and she didn't want to live. Why? Because she loved a man, and the man took her money, ran away and left her. And the man was called—'

'No!' said Meg. 'NO!'

'Yes, Meg, yes. He was called Mr Hollywood.'

'No!' shouted Meg. She began to cry.

'That's right, Miss Hutson,' said detective Keat quietly. 'To you, he gave the name Craig Winters. When Anna Vickers knew him, he was Carl Windser. But he liked all his . . . er . . . girlfriends to call him Mr Hollywood. He took nearly 50,000 dollars from Anna Vickers. And there was a girl before that . . .'

'No, it's not true!' Meg shouted.

'It *is* true, Meg,' said her father. 'Winters – Windser – gets all his money from rich men's daughters. Johnnie Vickers loved his daughter. He went to her house in Boston after she died. He read her letters, and learned about the money and the name Mr Hollywood. And when he came to my house, I told him about you, Meg. I said, "My

35

daughter's got a new boyfriend, and she calls him Mr Hollywood. I don't like him, but I can't stop her. She's going away to meet him next week, I think. What can I do?" Johnnie put his hand on my arm, and he said, "Don't be afraid for your daughter. I'm going to find that man – and stop him!"'

Meg said nothing. Her face was very white. For a minute or two nobody spoke, then detective Edmonds said:

'Vickers told us all about it, Miss Hutson. He followed you to Whistler, and saw you with—'

Nick began to understand. 'With me, in the café! And Meg called me Mr Hollywood!'

Howard Hutson looked at Nick. 'You're the travel writer guy, right?'

'Lortz. Nick Lortz,' said Nick. 'Vickers nearly killed me. He shot at me twice, and—'

But Howard Hutson was not very interested in Nick. He looked at his daughter again.

'How much money did you give him, Meg?' he said.

'I – I gave him 25,000 dollars,' said Meg. 'Only for two or three months, he said. Then he . . .' She began to cry again.

'Well, you can say goodbye to that money,' said Hutson angrily.

'What's going to happen to Vickers?' Nick asked detective Edmonds.

Meg said nothing.

'Hospital, I think,' said Edmonds. 'OK, he shot at you and about fifty people saw him. But he's not a well man. The doctors are going to put him away in a hospital.'

Howard Hutson stood up. 'OK, Meg, I'm going to take you home. My plane is waiting at the airport.'

Meg followed her father to the door, then she

remembered Nick and turned.

'I'm sorry,' she said. 'I got you into all this. I called you Mr Hollywood. That was wrong. But I didn't know—'

'It's OK,' said Nick. 'You know everything now. And it's better to learn it now, and not later. 50,000 dollars later.'

'I'm sorry I got you into all this.'

— 8 —

A nice smile

Nick took the evening ferry back to Vancouver. He was tired and hungry, so he went down to get some dinner in the ferry restaurant.

The restaurant was busy and there was only one free table. Nick sat down quickly and began to eat. 'I must get back to work tomorrow,' he thought, 'and forget about millionaires' daughters and men with guns.'

'Excuse me,' somebody said. 'Can I sit with you?'

'Excuse me. Can I sit with you?'

39

Nick looked up. There was a pretty girl next to his table. He got up.

'It – it's OK,' he said. 'You can have this table. I don't want it.' And he began to move away.

'Please don't go,' the girl said. 'Stay and finish your dinner.' She smiled at him. It was a nice smile.

But Nick knew all about nice smiles.

'I'm not hungry,' he said.

And he walked quickly out of the restaurant.

GLOSSARY

bar a room where people can buy and have drinks
blood blood is red and moves around inside the body
bridge something built high to go over a river or a road
busy with many things happening
café a place where people can buy and eat food and drink
city a big important town
crowd a lot of people
desk people in offices sit and work at desks
fall (past tense **fell**) to go down quickly from a high place
ferry a ship to carry cars and people
floor the part of a room which is under your feet
fly (past tense **flew**) to travel through the air (e.g. by aeroplane)
follow to go after someone or something
great wonderful, very good
guess to try to give the right answer when you don't know it
gun a thing that shoots out bullets to kill people
guy a man
kiss *(v)* to touch someone with your lips, to show love, or to
   say hello or goodbye
magazine a book with a paper cover which comes out every
   week, month, etc.
maybe perhaps
millionaire somebody who has a million pounds or dollars, or
   more
mountain a very big hill
movie a film which you see at a cinema
mystery something that you do not understand and cannot
   explain

outside not in something (a room, a building, etc.)

park *(n)* a garden or place in a town where people can walk, sit, play games, etc.

party a meeting of friends to eat, drink, talk, dance, etc.

point *(v)* to show with your finger where someone or something is

policeman the police are the men and women in a country who catch criminals, try to stop people doing wrong, etc.

police station an office of the police

pretty beautiful, nice to look at

pull to hold and move something towards you

push to move something away from you with your hands

restaurant a place where people can buy and eat meals

scream to cry out loudly, usually when you are afraid or hurt

shoot (past tense **shot**) to send a bullet from a gun to kill or hurt somebody

short not tall

shot *(n)* the bullet sent from a gun

shout *(v)* to call or cry out loudly and strongly

stranger somebody that you do not know

sure certain, knowing that something is true

tea a hot drink, often with sugar and milk or lemon

travel to visit other countries, cities, etc.

turn to move round

vacation a holiday, a time when you do not work and perhaps go travelling

waiter somebody who brings your food or drink in a restaurant or café

worried afraid that something is wrong or something bad is going to happen

Goodbye, Mr Hollywood

ACTIVITIES

Before Reading

1 Read the introduction on the first page of the book, and the back cover. How much do you know now about the story? Tick one of the boxes.

	YES	NO
1 This is a mystery story.	☐	☐
2 The story happens in the USA.	☐	☐
3 Nick gets a kiss from a beautiful girl in a café.	☐	☐
4 Nick met the girl three weeks ago.	☐	☐
5 The girl calls Nick 'Mr Hollywood'.	☐	☐
6 Nick knows the man with short white hair.	☐	☐
7 When Nick leaves the café, he forgets about the girl.	☐	☐

2 What is going to happen in the story? Can you guess? Tick one box for each sentence.

	YES	NO	PERHAPS
1 Nick tries to find the girl	☐	☐	☐
2 Somebody tries to kill Nick.	☐	☐	☐
3 Nick kills 'Mr Hollywood'.	☐	☐	☐
4 Nick gets a lot of money.	☐	☐	☐
5 Nick meets the man with short white hair.	☐	☐	☐

While Reading

Read Chapter 1 and answer these questions.

1 Who first saw the girl across the street?
2 What did Nick learn from the letter in the girl's bag?
3 The girl knew somebody called 'Mr Hollywood'. Why was he called that?
4 Who followed Nick when he left the café?
5 Who watched Nick from a hotel window?

Read Chapter 2, and then complete these sentences. Use one word for each gap.

1 Nick fell in front of a car because somebody _____ him.
2 In the hotel Nick read a _____ and saw a _____ of Jan.
3 She was Meg Hutson, the daughter of a _____.

Read Chapter 3. Choose the best question-word for these questions, and then answer them.

Who / Where / What
1 . . . noise did Nick hear in the park?
2 . . . did Nick find on the window of his car?
3 . . . did Nick go next?
4 . . . wrote down Nick's story?

ACTIVITIES: *While Reading*

Read Chapter 4. Are these sentences true (T) or false (F)? Change the false sentences into true ones.

1 The woman at the hotel desk was not interested in Nick's questions about a man with white hair.
2 It was a very small hotel.
3 Nick remembered the letter in the girl's bag.
4 Nick saw the man with white hair in a taxi.
5 A small girl ran in front of Nick in the hotel restaurant, and Nick ran into her.
6 The name of the man with white hair was Mr Hutson.

Read Chapter 5, and then put these sentences in the right order.

1 He saw Nick's car outside the hotel.
2 Nick took the ferry to Vancouver Island.
3 Then he came into the hotel, with a gun in his pocket.
4 She was in the hotel tea room with a man.
5 Then he went to the Empress Hotel in Victoria and asked for Meg Hutson.
6 But the man with white hair followed Nick to Vancouver Island.

Read Chapter 6. Who said this, and to whom?

1 'No, thanks. I'm with the two people over there.'
2 'Sometimes called Mr Hollywood?'

25

3 'I think he's a detective. And I think he's working for my father.'

4 'Tell – tell me about this man with white hair.'

5 'You're afraid of him. Why?'

6 'That's Mr Hollywood! That man there!'

7 'This is for Anna!'

Before you read Chapters 7 and 8, look at these sentences. Can you guess the best ending for each sentence?

1 Mr Vickers wants to kill Mr Hollywood because . . .

a) he likes to kill people.

b) Mr Hollywood killed or hurt someone in his family.

c) Mr Hollywood took all his money.

2 Anna is Mr Vickers' . . .

a) daughter.

b) sister.

c) wife.

3 Craig Winters . . .

a) dies.

b) goes to prison.

c) goes to hospital.

4 Mr Vickers . . .

a) dies.

b) goes to prison.

c) goes to hospital.

After Reading

1 **Read this newspaper report about the shooting at the Empress Hotel. There are 16 things wrong with it. Find the mistakes and correct them.**

This afternoon a gunman shot a woman in the Empress Hotel in Victoria. 'He walked past me and went into the television room,' said the woman behind the hotel desk. 'He was a short fat man with red hair.'

The man took a gun out of his bag and walked across to a table. A young woman at this table jumped to her feet and shouted, 'Mr Hollywood's not here!' A second young woman pushed over the tea table. The gunman shot three times and hit one of the young women in the leg.

Three waiters pulled the gunman down on to the floor. Soon after, the police arrived.

The gunman is Mr Nick Lortz. His daughter Meg died three months ago in San Francisco. She fell under a train.

Now choose the best headline for the report.

- MAN KILLED AT EMPRESS HOTEL
- SHOOTING AT THE EMPRESS
- WOMAN SHOT BY MYSTERY GUNMAN
- DINNER STOPS FOR GUNMAN

2 Match the people with the sentences. Then use the sentences to write a short description of each person. Use pronouns (*he, she, him, her*) and linking words (*but, and, because*) when you can.

Nick Lortz / Meg Hutson / Craig Winters / Howard Hutson / Johnnie Vickers

Example: *Nick met a girl in a café in Whistler. He didn't know her, but he . . .*

1 _Nick_ met a girl in a café in Whistler.
2 _____ was the daughter of a millionaire.
3 _____ used a lot of different names.
4 _____ was Meg's father.
5 _____ was the man with white hair.
6 _____ loved a man called Craig Winters.
7 _____ wanted to stop his daughter seeing 'Mr Hollywood'.
8 _Nick_ didn't know this girl.
9 _____ got all his money from rich men's daughters.
10 _____ thought that Nick was 'Mr Hollywood'.
11 _____ was happy to sit and talk with this girl.
12 _____ liked his girlfriends to call him 'Mr Hollywood'.
13 _____ gave Craig Winters 25,000 dollars.
14 _____ tried three times to kill Nick.
15 _____ knew Johnnie Vickers.

49

3 Here is a new illustration for the story. Find the best place in the story to put the picture, and answer these questions.

The picture goes on page _____.

1 Who are the two men in the picture?

2 Where are they?

3 What are they doing?

Now write a caption for the illustration.

Caption: _____

4 How does Craig Winters get 25,000 dollars out of Meg? Put their telephone conversation in the right order, and write in the names. Craig speaks first (number 5).

1 _____ 'Why? What's the matter?'

2 _____ 'No, no. I can't take money from you, Meg.'

3 _____ 'Craig, I'm fine. But I want to see you. When can we meet?'

4 _____ 'Meg, you're wonderful. How about 25,000? Just for two or three months, you understand.'

5 _____ 'Hi, Meg. How are you?'

6 _____ 'It's my mother. I can't leave her because her legs are very bad and she can't walk far. She needs a new car, but I don't have the money just now.'

7 _____ 'Of course you can! How much do you need? 15,000? 20,000? Just tell me. You can have it tomorrow.'

8 _____ 'I don't know. I want to see you too, but things aren't easy at the moment.'

9 _____ 'But Craig, that's easy! I can give you the money.'

5 Use words from (1) with words from (2) to make some new titles for this story. How many titles can you make? Which ones are best for the story?

1 a / the / at / in / with / of / and / hello

2 café / daughter / girl / hair / Hollywood / man / Mr / meeting / mystery / nice / rich / smile / Whistler / white / Winters / wrong

ABOUT THE AUTHOR

John Escott worked in business before becoming a writer. Since then he has written many books for readers of all ages, but enjoys writing crime and mystery thrillers most of all. He was born in Somerset, in the west of England, but now lives in Bournemouth on the south coast. When he is not working, he likes looking for long-forgotten books in small back-street bookshops, watching old Hollywood films on video, and walking for miles along empty beaches.

He has written or retold many stories for the Oxford Bookworms Library. His original stories include *Dead Man's Island* and *Agatha Christie, Woman of Mystery* (both at Stage 2).

OXFORD BOOKWORMS LIBRARY

Classics • Crime & Mystery • Factfiles • Fantasy & Horror
Human Interest • Playscripts • Thriller & Adventure
True Stories • World Stories

The OXFORD BOOKWORMS LIBRARY provides enjoyable reading in English, with a wide range of classic and modern fiction, non-fiction, and plays. It includes original and adapted texts in seven carefully graded language stages, which take learners from beginner to advanced level. An overview is given on the next pages.

All Stage 1 titles are available as audio recordings, as well as over eighty other titles from Starter to Stage 6. All Starters and many titles at Stages 1 to 4 are specially recommended for younger learners. Every Bookworm is illustrated, and Starters and Factfiles have full-colour illustrations.

The OXFORD BOOKWORMS LIBRARY also offers extensive support. Each book contains an introduction to the story, notes about the author, a glossary, and activities. Additional resources include tests and worksheets, and answers for these and for the activities in the books. There is advice on running a class library, using audio recordings, and the many ways of using Oxford Bookworms in reading programmes. Resource materials are available on the website <www.oup.com/bookworms>.

The *Oxford Bookworms Collection* is a series for advanced learners. It consists of volumes of short stories by well-known authors, both classic and modern. Texts are not abridged or adapted in any way, but carefully selected to be accessible to the advanced student.

You can find details and a full list of titles in the *Oxford Bookworms Library Catalogue* and *Oxford English Language Teaching Catalogues*, and on the website <www.oup.com/bookworms>.

THE OXFORD BOOKWORMS LIBRARY
GRADING AND SAMPLE EXTRACTS

STARTER • 250 HEADWORDS
present simple – present continuous – imperative –
can/cannot, must – *going to* (future) – simple gerunds ...

Her phone is ringing – but where is it?

Sally gets out of bed and looks in her bag. No phone. She looks under the bed. No phone. Then she looks behind the door. There is her phone. Sally picks up her phone and answers it. *Sally's Phone*

STAGE 1 • 400 HEADWORDS
... past simple – coordination with *and, but, or* –
subordination with *before, after, when, because, so* ...

I knew him in Persia. He was a famous builder and I worked with him there. For a time I was his friend, but not for long. When he came to Paris, I came after him – I wanted to watch him. He was a very clever, very dangerous man. *The Phantom of the Opera*

STAGE 2 • 700 HEADWORDS
... present perfect – *will* (future) – *(don't) have to, must not, could* –
comparison of adjectives – simple *if* clauses – past continuous –
tag questions – *ask/tell* + infinitive ...

While I was writing these words in my diary, I decided what to do. I must try to escape. I shall try to get down the wall outside. The window is high above the ground, but I have to try. I shall take some of the gold with me – if I escape, perhaps it will be helpful later. *Dracula*

... should, may – present perfect continuous – *used to* – past perfect –
causative – relative clauses – indirect statements ...

Of course, it was most important that no one should see
Colin, Mary, or Dickon entering the secret garden. So Colin
gave orders to the gardeners that they must all keep away
from that part of the garden in future. *The Secret Garden*

STAGE 4 • 1400 HEADWORDS

... past perfect continuous – passive (simple forms) –
would conditional clauses – indirect questions –
relatives with *where/when* – gerunds after prepositions/phrases ...

I was glad. Now Hyde could not show his face to the world
again. If he did, every honest man in London would be proud
to report him to the police. *Dr Jekyll and Mr Hyde*

STAGE 5 • 1800 HEADWORDS

... future continuous – future perfect –
passive (modals, continuous forms) –
would have conditional clauses – modals + perfect infinitive ...

If he had spoken Estella's name, I would have hit him. I was so
angry with him, and so depressed about my future, that I could
not eat the breakfast. Instead I went straight to the old house.
Great Expectations

STAGE 6 • 2500 HEADWORDS

... passive (infinitives, gerunds) – advanced modal meanings –
clauses of concession, condition

When I stepped up to the piano, I was confident. It was as if I
knew that the prodigy side of me really did exist. And when I
started to play, I was so caught up in how lovely I looked that
I didn't worry how I would sound. *The Joy Luck Club*

White Death

TIM VICARY

Sarah Harland is nineteen, and she is in prison. At the airport, they find heroin in her bag. So, now she is waiting to go to court. If the court decides that it was her heroin, then she must die.

She says she did not do it. But if she did not, who did? Only two people can help Sarah: her mother, and an old boyfriend who does not love her now. Can they work together? Can they find the real criminal before it is too late?

Sister Love and Other Crime Stories

JOHN ESCOTT

Some sisters are good friends, some are not. Sometimes there is more hate in a family than there is love. Karin is beautiful and has lots of men friends, but she can be very unkind to her sister Marcia. Perhaps when they were small, there was love between them, but that was a long time ago.

They say that everybody has one crime in them. Perhaps they only take an umbrella that does not belong to them. Perhaps they steal from a shop, perhaps they get angry and hit someone, perhaps they kill . . .